HISTORY & GEOGRAPHY 507
DEPRESSION AND WAR

Introduction |3

1. The Great Depression 4
Despair |5
New Deal |8
The World Goes to War |13
Isolation Ended |18
Self Test 1 |22

2. The War in Europe 25
The Home Front |26
Turning Point |30
D-Day |34
Holocaust |36
Self Test 2 |38

3. The War in the Pacific 41
Pacific Turning Point |43
Island Hopping |46
Final Victory |50
Self Test 3 |55

LIFEPAC Test |Pull-out

Author:
Theresa Buskey, J.D.

Editor:
Alan Christopherson, M.S.

Media Credits:
Page 3: © Matt Gibson, iStock, Thinkstock; **4:** © Leonard Maiorani, iStock, Thinkstock; **5:** Harris & Ewing, Library of Congress; **6:** © Brand X Pictures, Stockbyte, Thinkstock; © Ahmad Atwah, iStock, Thinkstock; **7:** © Daniel Villeneuve, iStock, Thinkstock; **9:** © Greg Morrow, iStock, Thinkstock; Elias Goldensky, Library of Congress; **10:** © tankbmb, iStock, Thinkstock; © Comstock Images, Stockbyte, Thinkstock; **11:** © Zerbor, iStock, Thinkstock; © Fox Photos, Valueline, Thinkstock; **14:** © Glam-Y, iStock, Thinkstock; **14, 16:** © Photos.com, Thinkstock; **15:** © Office of War Information, Library of Congress; **18, 34, 35:** © Dorling Kindersley, Thinkstock; **19:** © Phdb, iStock, Thinkstock; **20:** © Latham Jenkins, iStock, Thinkstock; **25:** © abadonian, iStock, Thinkstock; **26:** © Tony Baggett, iStock, Thinkstock; **27:** © Tamara Murray, iStock, Thinkstock; **28:** © Aloysius Patrimonio, Hemera, Thinkstock; © Woodkern, iStock, Thinkstock; **30:** © Oleg Kulakov, Hemera, Thinkstock; **31:** T4c. Messerlin, Army; **35:** Sgt Hewitt, No 5 Army Film & Photographic Unit, Imperial War Museum; **36:** © Ingram Publishing, Thinkstock; **41:** © Purestock, Thinkstock; **43:** © Ian Ilot, iStock, Thinkstock; **44:** © Elenarts, iStock, Thinkstock; **45:** © Aloysius Patrimonio, Hemera, Thinkstock; **46:** © EdenExit1, iStock, Thinkstock; **47:** © Angus McBride, Thinkstock; © Gary Blakeley, Thinkstock; **50:** Frank Gatteri, United States Army Signal Corps.; **51:** © Denis Zorin, iStock, Thinkstock; **52:** © Purestock, Thinkstock; **53:** © Stockbyte, Thinkstock.

All maps in this book © Map Resources, unless otherwise stated.

Alpha Omega
PUBLICATIONS

804 N. 2nd Ave. E.
Rock Rapids, IA 51246-1759

DEPRESSION AND WAR

The Stock Market Crash of 1929 started the Great Depression. This was the largest, deepest, and hardest depression in American history. Millions of people were out of work, not just in America, but all over the world. A new president tried all kinds of things to end the depression, but it was World War II that finally brought jobs and prosperity back to America again.

The Second World War started in 1939 when Germany invaded Poland. Like World War I, America was isolationist and refused to get involved. However, when the Japanese (allies of Germany) attacked American soil in Hawaii in 1941, America got involved. The united American people gave the supplies and men needed to defeat the dictators and win the war.

This LIFEPAC® will discuss both the Great Depression and the biggest war in the history of the world, World War II.

Objectives

Read these objectives. The objectives tell you what you will be able to do when you have successfully completed this LIFEPAC. Each section will list according to the numbers below what objectives will be met in that section. When you have finished this LIFEPAC, you should be able to:

1. Describe the problems of the Great Depression.
2. Describe the New Deal and FDR's actions as president.
3. Describe World War II: especially its beginning, turning point, and events that led to the end of the war.
4. Describe American participation and strategy in World War II.
5. Name the leaders of World War II.

1. THE GREAT DEPRESSION

The Great Depression was a huge shock to the nation. The Roaring Twenties had been so prosperous that no one expected such poverty to follow, but it did. Millions of people had no jobs, no homes, and little food. The nation was filled with despair.

In 1932 the nation chose a new president, Democrat Franklin Delano Roosevelt (a distant cousin of Theodore Roosevelt). Franklin Roosevelt (FDR) promised the nation a "New Deal." He tried all kinds of things to restart businesses and get jobs and food for people. His New Deal gave people hope and helped ease the worst losses of the depression. However, the depression did not end until 1942.

War broke out in Europe again in 1939. The U.S. was still isolationist and tried to stay out of this war. However, as more and more of Europe and Asia fell to the dictators of the Axis Powers, Americans became concerned. FDR did everything he could to help Britain, which was fighting alone in Europe. The U.S. got involved when it began manufacturing needed war supplies for Great Britain. This action created jobs in America and finally ended the Great Depression in 1942.

Objectives

Review these objectives. When you have completed this section, you should be able to:

1. Describe the problems of the Great Depression.
2. Describe the New Deal and FDR's actions as president.
3. Describe World War II: especially its beginning, turning point, and events that led up to the end of the war.
5. Name the leaders of World War II.

Vocabulary

Study these new words. Learning the meanings of these words is a good study habit and will improve your understanding of this LIFEPAC.

aggression (ə gresh′ ən). The first step or move in an attack or quarrel; action by the person or nation starting a war or fight.

appease (ə pēz). To make calm or quiet; to give someone what they want to make them calm or quiet.

charity (char′ ə tē). A fund or organization for helping the sick, the poor or the helpless.

veteran (vet′ ər ən). A person who has served in the armed forces.

violation (vī′ ə lā shən). A breaking of a law, rule, agreement, promise, or instruction.

Note: *All vocabulary words in this LIFEPAC appear in* **boldface** *print the first time they are used. If you are unsure of the meaning when you are reading, study the definitions given.*

Pronunciation Key: hat, āge, cãre, fär; let, ēqual, tėrm; it, īce; hot, ōpen, ôrder; oil; out; cup, put, rüle; child; long; thin; /ŦH/ for then; /zh/ for measure; /u/ or /ə/ represents /a/ in about, /e/ in taken, /i/ in pencil, /o/ in lemon, and /u/ in circus.

Despair

Hoovervilles. Herbert Hoover was president when the stock market crashed in 1929, starting the Great Depression. Hoover was an engineer who was famous for getting aid to people who were starving in Europe during and after World War I. He was a good organizer and a very popular president until the depression began. Everyone blamed him for the depression, and he became one of the most unpopular presidents in American history.

| Herbert Hoover

The Great Depression destroyed the Roaring Twenties idea that America would be rich forever. At its worst point in 1933, one out of every four people did not have a job. That meant one out of every four families had no money for food, clothes, or housing. Many of the people who did have jobs had their pay reduced so that they had less money to spend for what they needed. Many of the people who had bought on credit could not pay for their goods. Hard working people all over the nation lost everything. The nation became poorer and poorer.

Thousands of men wandered around the country searching for any work they could find. They slept covered with old newspapers they called "Hoover blankets." Communities of shacks made of cardboard, wood, and tin were called "Hoovervilles." People sold apples and shined shoes to get a few cents for a meal. When they could not earn even a few cents, they stood in long lines at **charity** or town aid stations to get a free piece of bread or bowl of soup.

| People often stood in long lines for a free bowl of soup.

Things on the farms had already been bad in the 1920s. Conditions got worse during the Great Depression. Prices for food fell so low that farmers could not make enough money to pay for seed or for shipping crops to market! Droughts in the Great Plains dried up the soil and created huge dust storms. Those rich lands became known as the "Dust Bowl." Thousands of farmers lost their land, packed all their belongings in a car or cart, and traveled the country looking for work.

| Dust storms wiped away crops and drove people from their homes in the Midwest.

Thousands of banks failed between 1929 and 1933. People began to distrust banks and would withdraw their money from them. Without money, banks were forced to close. Every bank that closed caused hundreds of people to lose their savings. People who had worked hard and saved for years were left with nothing.

Herbert Hoover, a Republican, was not able to stop the Great Depression. He believed that American businesses were strong and should put themselves back to work, but this time they could not. The American people wanted a president who would use government money to feed people, create jobs, and help businesses. However, the U.S. government had never done this in any of the many depressions or panics that had hurt the nation in the past. Hoover would not use government money to give to people because he believed he could not. He did try some new things to help the people, but it was not enough to please a desperate nation. He quickly became a hated man.

Bonus Army. The soldiers who had fought in World War I were among the many Americans suffering in the depression. In 1924 the U.S. government had promised them a bonus for their service during the war. They were supposed to get the bonus in 1945. However, these men had no jobs and wanted their bonus right away. They were not willing to wait thirteen years when their families were hungry now.

In 1932 about 20,000 ex-soldiers marched on Washington. They came to ask Congress to give them their bonus right away, because they needed it so badly. They called themselves the Bonus Expeditionary Force. (Remember the U.S. Army in World War I was the American Expeditionary Force.) The press called them the Bonus Army. They built a huge Hooverville in the capital and waited for Congress to grant their demand.

| Veterans marched on Washington and demanded their bonuses.

Congress refused to give the bonuses out early. Much of the Bonus Army, however, refused to leave. So, after some fighting broke out, Hoover sent the army in to remove the camp. The army commander, Douglas MacArthur, treated the **veterans** harshly, using tear gas and weapons to drive them out of Washington. Then, the camp was burned. The American public felt that the veterans had been treated unfairly, and they blamed Herbert Hoover.

FDR. The Republican party had been a supporter of businesses for a long time. By 1932 the American people believed big business and the Republicans had caused the Great Depression. Herbert Hoover ran for president again in 1932, but he did not have a chance. Anyone could have beaten him. The man the Democrats chose to run for president in 1932 was Franklin Delano Roosevelt, the governor of New York. He won easily.

FDR believed the government should use its money to fix the depression. He had used state money to help people in New York as governor. He was willing to try all kinds of new things to end the depression. He was very good at convincing people to trust him. He gave the country hope with his policies which he called the "New Deal."

Answer these questions.

1.1   Which president was blamed for the Great Depression?

_____

1.2   What did the veterans call themselves who marched on Washington for their bonuses?

_____

1.3   What fraction of people were out of work at the worst of the depression?

_____

1.4   What happened to thousands of men who could not find work?

_____

_____

1.5   What was the Great Plains called because of the drought there?

_____

1.6   Who did Herbert Hoover believe should fix the depression? _____

1.7   What happened to thousands of banks between 1929 and 1933?

_____

1.8   What happened to the Bonus Army camp in Washington?_____

_____

1.9   Who was elected president in 1932? _____

1.10   FDR's policies for the depression were called what? _____

1.11   What was a Hooverville? _____

_____

1.12   What was a Hoover blanket? _____

1.13   What did Herbert Hoover believe he could not do with government money?

_____

New Deal

Policy change. Franklin Delano Roosevelt's New Deal was a huge change in government policy. Today we expect the government to provide for people who lose their jobs, cannot work, or cannot pay for a doctor. That was not true before the Great Depression. The government never tried to take care of people who were in trouble before that time. It also did very little to control or help businesses except for laws to prevent abuses like child labor or unfair prices on the railroad.

The New Deal was the first time in American history that the government took responsibility for the businesses and work of the nation. Before that time people all over the country believed the government had no right to do that. They believed that taxes taken from the people could not be used to help specific people in trouble or interfere with the freedom of businesses to do as they wanted. However, the crisis of the Great Depression changed that. Now people wanted the government's help, and FDR was determined to give it.

The New Deal had three goals: relief, recovery, and reform. Relief was to provide people with the food, clothing, and shelter they needed to live. Recovery was to get people working and buying goods again. Reform was to change the laws so that such an awful depression could never happen to America again.

The Hundred Days. At his inauguration Roosevelt calmed the nation with his hopeful speech. He told the people that they had "nothing to fear except fear itself." FDR then called Congress into session to go to work. The now Democratic Congress gave the president anything he wanted to try to combat the depression. The result was a huge pile of new laws. This time of rapid action was called the "Hundred Days."

Roosevelt's first action was to declare a bank holiday. He closed all the banks in the country for a week. He promised that only the banks that were safe would be allowed to reopen. People believed him. When the banks reopened, people stopped taking their money out. Very few banks failed after that.

The new Congress passed dozens of laws creating organizations to help people and businesses. Most of the organizations were known by their letters, like the Civilian Conservation Corp, called the CCC. Thus, Roosevelt's laws were sometimes called alphabet soup!

The Civilian Conservation Corp was the most famous and most popular of the relief organizations. It took young men who had no jobs and put them into military-like units. They were put to work building trails in national parks, replanting forests, building roads, and fighting forest fires. They worked hard and

| Franklin Delano Roosevelt

| Replanting forests was one of the CCC's projects.

were paid very little, but they got a place to sleep, food to eat, and a little money to send home.

The president created other relief organizations. The Federal Emergency Relief Administration (FERA) gave money to states and cities for food, clothing, and shelter. The Civil Works Administration (CWA), the Public Works Administration (PWA), and the Work Progress Administration (WPA) created jobs for people. This was done by having the government hire them to build roads, parks, dams, or buildings. These put millions of people to work on temporary jobs.

| The TVA built dams and brought benefits to the Tennessee River Valley, particularly the Norris Dam (pictured).

FDR hoped that the public works jobs would give people money to spend on goods. Then, the factories would start hiring people to make the goods. This was called "priming the pump," putting money into the nation to get it producing money again, like water sometimes had to be put into a hand pump to get it to pump water again.

One of the biggest public works projects was the Tennessee Valley Authority (TVA). The TVA's job was to build dams and produce electricity on the Tennessee River, one of the poorest places in the country. The TVA transformed the Tennessee River Valley. It controlled flooding, reduced soil erosion, provided jobs, built new homes, and made the entire region prosper.

To encourage recovery, the Agricultural Adjustment Act (AAA) helped farmers get better prices for their crops. The National Industrial Recovery Act (NIRA) tried to set up rules to help the nation's business get going again. All of these alphabet agencies helped by giving people jobs, some money, and hope. However, they did not end the depression.

FDR also passed some reform laws. The Securities and Exchange Commission (SEC) was created to control the stock market. The Federal Deposit Insurance Corporation (FDIC) was set up to protect deposits in banks. So, people could know that if the bank failed they would still get their money back because it was **insured**. The Social Security Act took money from everyone's wages to pay for workers who retired or could not work. The National Labor Relations Board (NLRB) was set up to enforce fair work laws and protect unions.

| Social Security pays retirees and people who cannot work.

The bad thing about all these alphabet organizations was how much they cost. The U.S. government did not have enough money to pay for all of it, so they borrowed the money. This is called *deficit spending*, spending money that creates debt. Once this kind of spending started, it was hard to stop. The U.S. government has usually continued to get deeper and deeper into debt since the Great Depression.

Good Neighbor Policy. Franklin D. Roosevelt also changed America's foreign policy. The United States had been overbearing with the other American continent nations since the Spanish-American War. FDR modified American foreign policy to be friendlier in the way it dealt with its close neighbors. American soldiers were taken out of Central America. Some controls over Cuba and Panama were ended. The U.S. finally began to treat the other nations of the Western Hemisphere with equality and respect. It was called the Good Neighbor Policy.

| The Good Neighbor Policy made the U.S. friendlier to its neighbors.

End of the New Deal. The nation was desperate when FDR was first elected, and Congress did anything he wanted. However, that began to change in 1936, after he was re-elected as president for a second term. Roosevelt made a serious mistake in 1937 when he tried to control the Supreme Court.

The Court had thrown out several of the New Deal laws. FDR tried to add six new justices who would agree with his policies. However, Congress refused to go along with his "court-packing plan." The fight over the idea hurt FDR's support in Congress. He could not get the Congress to agree with him as easily after that.

| Women working in a factory production line

Another thing that hurt Roosevelt's power was that the depression got worse again in 1937. However, it was not as bad as it had been in 1933, and things did improve the following year, but even with all of Roosevelt's new laws and plans, one out of six people was still without a job at the beginning of 1940. It was World War II that finally provided enough jobs to end the Great Depression.

Name the item, event, person, or thing.

1.14   The first time that the government took responsibility for business and work:

_____

1.15   FDR's foreign policy in the American hemisphere:

_____

1.16   The three goals of the New Deal:

_____

1.17   The CCC, gave conservation jobs to young men:

_____

1.18   The SEC, controlled the stock market:

_____

1.19   The time at the beginning of the New Deal when many new laws were passed:

_____

1.20   When the government spends more money than it has, creating debt:

_____

1.21   FDR's first action as president:

_____

1.22   An important public works organization, the WPA:

_____

1.23   Organization to get electricity from the Tennessee River, the TVA:

_____

1.24   Emergency relief for people, the FERA:

_____

1.25   Organization to enforce fair work laws, the NLRB:

_____

1.26   Congress refused to agree to add six more people to this in 1937:

_____

1.27   This finally ended the Great Depression:

_____

The World Goes to War

Japan. Japan was a powerful nation by 1940. Just after the Civil War in America (1861–1865), the Japanese government began to make its nation into an industrial power. They also began to build up their army and navy. Once they had a modern military, the Japanese Empire began to conquer neighboring lands in Asia. It conquered Korea in 1905 and Germany's colonies in the Far East during World War I. The military became very powerful in Japan because of its success.

Japan was ruled by an emperor whose family had ruled for hundreds of years. However, the military was the real power in Japan after 1936, and they wanted conquest.

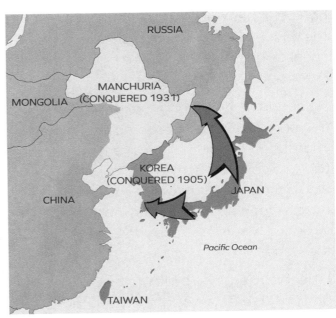

| Japan's aggression against Korea and Manchuria

They began in 1931 by capturing Manchuria, part of northern China. The League of Nations was not able to stop them. The League's failure ended any chance of controlling aggression by having the nations act together against it. It also demonstrated that the free nations of the world were not willing to go to war to stop aggression. There were several new, conquest-hungry dictators who were delighted to learn that.

Italy. A dictator in Italy named Benito Mussolini took control of the government in 1922. He was called *El Duce* (The Leader). He paid close attention when the Japanese succeeded in taking Manchuria without anyone trying to stop them. In 1935 the Italian army attacked and conquered Ethiopia in northern Africa. Again, the League of Nations and the powerful democracies did nothing to stop him.

Germany. Soon after World War I Germany had been hit by a time of rapidly rising prices called *hyper-inflation*. Prices went up so fast that baskets of money were needed to buy bread or shoes. Businesses would pay their workers twice a day and let them go buy things at lunchtime because the prices would be higher by evening! Later, Germany was hit hard by the Great Depression. It still had huge war debts, and its lands near France were still occupied by the French army. The people were desperate, and they did not get an elected leader like Franklin Roosevelt. Instead, they got Adolf Hitler.

Hitler was the leader of the Nazi Party in Germany. He believed the Germans were a superior people, a master race, better than the people of other nations, especially the Jews. He believed the Germans needed to conquer Europe to get room for themselves. He said that Germany had been betrayed by the Treaty of Versailles and that all of the problems of the nation had been caused by Jews and the Treaty. He was a great public speaker, and people followed him. He promised to make Germany great again.

Hitler and his Nazi Party took control of the government of Germany in 1933. He ordered people who spoke against him imprisoned and killed. His government attacked Jews in Germany, taking away their homes and businesses. Eventually, Hitler would order the Jews arrested and killed in huge camps called *concentration camps*. The symbol of Nazi Germany was the *swastika*, which is still considered a symbol of hatred throughout the world.

| Hitler killed 6 million Jews before he was stopped.

Hitler also began to build up the German army and air force. This was not lawful under the Treaty of Versailles, but no one was willing to stop him. In fact, the nations of Europe were so desperate to avoid war that they appeased him.

Britain and France appeased Hitler by giving him what he wanted, more land. They hoped he would be satisfied with a little, when he really wanted all of Europe. All they did was give him more power which he would use later to attack them. Appeasement of the dictator was not a very smart thing to do.

Hitler began his aggression in 1936 by sending his new army into the Rhineland, the land near France. This was a **violation** of the Treaty of Versailles. It threatened France, but France did not take any action. They did not want another war. In 1938 Hitler took Austria, which was a German-speaking land. That same year he demanded a part of Czechoslovakia in which many German people lived. France and Great Britain agreed to give it to him at the Munich Conference in 1938. Early in 1939 he conquered the rest of Czechoslovakia.

| Hitler (on right) and Benito Mussolini

By this time, France and Great Britain began to realize that Hitler was not going to stop. They stopped appeasing him. They told Germany that they would go to war if Hitler invaded Poland, which he wanted next.

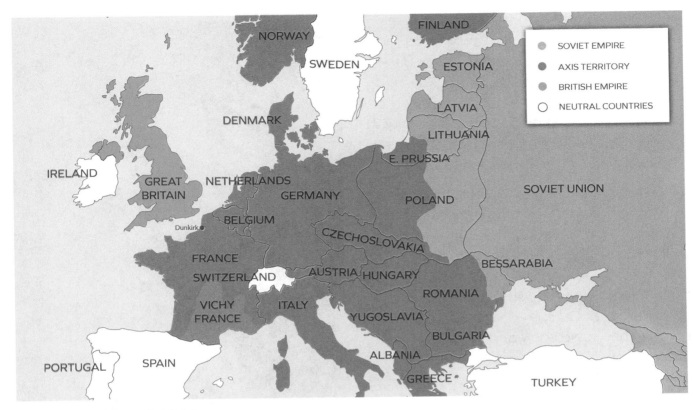

| Europe in May of 1941

Hitler hated communists, but he loved power more. In 1939 the Nazi dictator signed a secret treaty with Joseph Stalin, the communist dictator of Russia (called the Soviet Union then). Stalin and Hitler promised not to attack each other. They also agreed to divide Poland. Germany invaded Poland in September of 1939; that was the beginning of World War II because France and Britain declared war.

Europe Falls. The German army used a new way of fighting in World War II—it was called *blitzkrieg*, lightning war. They used speed and surprise. Soldiers with cars, motorcycles, tanks, and mobile guns moved quickly across the country. They wanted to prevent their enemies from setting up trenches like they had in World War I. It worked. Poland was conquered in a few weeks. The Soviet Union took the eastern part of Poland, and the western part of Germany.

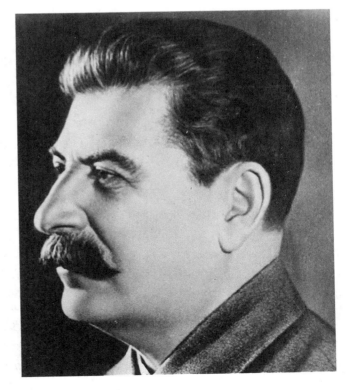

| Joseph Stalin

Hitler moved again in 1940. The Nazi army conquered Denmark and Norway in April. In May he took Belgium, Luxembourg, and the Netherlands in just a few days. The British army that was trying to defend Belgium and France was trapped at Dunkirk on the English Channel. It would have been captured except for what is called the "Miracle of Dunkirk."

When the people of Great Britain heard that their army was trapped across the channel at Dunkirk, they acted quickly. Every ship that could be found was sent across the channel to get them. Sailing ships, tugboats, fishing boats, and navy ships swarmed to the beaches at Dunkirk. They loaded all the soldiers they could carry and took them to England. The German air force tried to sink the ships, but there were too many of them. Over 300,000 soldiers were rescued in just over a week. Belgium and France were lost, but the British army survived and would return to fight another day.

| British evacuation at Dunkirk

Hitler attacked France in May of 1940. The French army quickly collapsed under the blitzkrieg. The German army took the French capital of Paris in June. That same month, France surrendered. Germany occupied the northern two-thirds of the country. The French kept control of a small piece of the country in the south, called Vichy France (after its new capital). Great Britain was the only enemy still fighting Germany in Europe. By this time, Germany, Italy, and Japan had formed an alliance called the Berlin-Rome-Tokyo Axis. They were called the Axis Powers for short.

Hitler expected Great Britain to surrender; but under the leadership of Winston Churchill, their prime minister, the proud British refused. They continued to fight even as the German army dropped thousands of bombs on their cities, reducing them to rubble. Eventually, Hitler realized Britain was not giving up, and he turned his attention to the rest of Europe.

Nazi Germany conquered Yugoslavia in April of 1941. That same month another German army conquered Greece which the Italians had been unsuccessfully trying to take. The island of Crete was taken by the Nazis in May. In June of 1941, Hitler invaded the Soviet Union, in spite of his treaty with Stalin. They advanced rapidly, killing thousands of Soviet soldiers. It looked like Hitler might take all of Europe, and the United States still had not entered the war.

Complete these sentences.

1.28 _____ was the dictator of Italy, _____ was the dictator of Germany, and _____ was the dictator of the Soviet Union.

1.29 The prime minister of Great Britain in World War II was _____ .

1.30 The symbol of Nazi Germany was the _____ .

1.31 The Nazi's new way of fighting was called _____ .

1.32 World War II began when Germany invaded _____ .

1.33 The small piece of France left after June of 1940 was called _____ .

1.34 The rescue of the British army across the English Channel by many British ships in May of 1940 was called the "Miracle of _____ ."

1.35 Hitler was appeased at the Conference in 1938 when Britain and France gave him part of _____ .

1.36 Hitler believed the Germans were a _____ race, especially better that the _____ people.

1.37 The League of Nations did not stop Japan when it invaded _____ in 1931 nor Italy when it invaded _____ in 1935.

1.38 By June of 1940, only _____ was still fighting Germany in Europe.

1.39 The alliance between Germany, Italy, and Japan was called the _____ .

1.40 In June of 1941, Hitler ignored his treaty with Stalin and invaded _____ .

Isolation Ended

Neutrality. The United States had returned to isolationism after World War I. The nation was determined not to get into any more foreign wars, especially as it continued to fight the Great Depression at home. In fact, in the 1930s Congress passed several Neutrality Laws that forbade America to trade with nations at war. Congress hoped that would keep the U.S. out of war because its ships would not be sunk as in World War I.

However, Roosevelt and most of the American people realized that Hitler and the Axis Powers were dangerous. When Japan invaded China in 1937, the U.S. continued to send weapons to China in spite of the law. When Germany invaded Poland, Roosevelt was determined to help Great Britain. Congress agreed, allowing the Allies (Britain and France) to buy war goods for cash in America; but they had to be carried to Europe on Allied ships.

After the fall of France, America began to prepare itself and to help Britain even more. A draft law was passed, and money was spent to improve the navy. President Roosevelt gave Britain some old navy ships they really needed in exchange for navy bases in the Atlantic. But the U.S. still refused to consider getting into the war.

In the middle of the crisis in 1940, America held an election for president. FDR broke a tradition that went back to George Washington when he ran for a third term that year. He was re-elected and would win again in 1944. He was the only U.S. president ever elected to serve four terms in office. (The Constitution was changed in 1951 to forbid more than two terms.)

After his election in 1940, Roosevelt announced his biggest plan yet to aid the Allies. It was called *Lend-Lease*. Basically, the plan allowed America to lend war supplies like guns and tanks to Britain. They would be returned or paid for after the war. This meant that Britain could have all the supplies America could produce until the war was won. America was willing to give all that was needed except her own soldiers. The Soviet Union was allowed to join Lend-Lease in 1941, after Germany invaded and the Soviets joined the Allies.

Winston Churchill and President Roosevelt worked closely together and became friends during World War II. In August of 1941 they met off the coast of Canada to discuss the war. Together they wrote a list of goals for peace. It was called the Atlantic Charter.

| Winston Churchill making the 'V' for victory sign

Two main points of the charter were:

1. All people should have the right to choose their own form of government, and
2. A new "League of Nations" should be created in order to maintain world-wide peace.

Japan. Japan, in the meantime, had attacked the rest of China. In September of 1940, Japan invaded French Indochina (Vietnam). However, the nation of Japan had no oil. It had to buy all its oil to fuel its army and navy from the United States. The U.S. had foolishly continued to sell Japan both oil and metals into 1940. However, as Japanese aggression continued, the U.S. finally cut off all sales of these goods to Japan in 1941.

Japan had to have oil to continue its conquests in Asia. There were supplies of oil in southeast Asia. So, rather than withdraw from China, Japan decided to get those supplies for itself. First, however, the Japanese military government believed it had to destroy the U.S. fleet in the Pacific to prevent it from stopping them.

Pearl Harbor. December 7, 1941 was a quiet Sunday at Pearl Harbor, Hawaii. The harbor was a large U.S. navy base. It was the home base of the Pacific fleet. On that day most of the Pacific fleet of modern battleships, eight of them, were tied up in the harbor. By God's grace, the three aircraft carriers were out at sea.

Unknown to the relaxed crews and visitors, a Japanese fleet was nearby. Early in the morning, the Japanese fleet launched airplanes for a surprise attack on the harbor. The completely unexpected attack came just before 8:00 in the morning. No one knew anything about it until the bomb explosions began killing people and destroying things.

| The attack on Pearl Harbor "awakened a sleeping giant."

The attack on Pearl was a huge Japanese victory. All eight of the U.S. battleships were sunk or heavily damaged. The *Oklahoma* and the *Utah* tipped upside down, trapping some of their crew. The *California* and the *West Virginia* sank, still tied to their docks. The *Nevada* tried to escape to sea, but was hit on the way out and had to be driven on to a beach to avoid sinking. A dozen other navy ships were also damaged or sunk.

About half of the American sailors killed that day were on board the battleship *Arizona*. A 1,760-pound bomb designed to go through metal plates hit the ship early in the attack. The bomb caused an explosion in the room where the ammunition was stored. The ship sunk in less than nine minutes, killing 1,177 of the men on board.

About 300 American planes were destroyed, most of them still on the ground. Over 2,000 Americans were killed. No one was ready at the anti-aircraft guns when the attack began. Much of the ammunition for the guns was locked up so the men could not get to it quickly. The Japanese ships escaped without a scratch, and less than 30 Japanese planes were shot down. The attack lasted almost two hours.

The victory was tremendous, but incomplete. The three massive aircraft carriers, the *Lexington*, the *Enterprise,* and the *Saratoga*, were safe. They would be incredibly important for America during the first year and a half of the war. Most of the fuel for the navy that was stored in the harbor was not hit. Damage to the harbor was repaired quickly. Several of the battleships were also raised from the water, repaired, and sent back into battle.

The victory at Pearl Harbor probably cost Japan the war. Due to delays in Washington, the Japanese ambassador did not deliver his message declaring war until *after the attack had begun*. The sly, sneaky attack on American soil without a declaration of war angered the nation. Isolationism ended on December 7, 1941. The next day, FDR called it "a date that will live in infamy" when he asked Congress to declare war. The nation went to bed on December 6th wanting to stay out of the war. It arose on December 7th united, determined to fight and win at any cost.

| The Arizona Memorial sits above the sunken *USS Arizona* in Pearl Harbor.

Give the information requested.

1.41   The only U.S. president elected to serve four terms:

_____

1.42   Roosevelt's plan to give the Allies what they needed to fight after 1940:

_____

1.43   The peace goals of FDR and Winston Churchill: _____

1.44   Ship sunk at Pearl Harbor with the loss of 1,177 men: _____

1.45   "A date that will live in infamy…" _____

1.46   Supplies Japan needed from America in 1940: _____

1.47   The important ships that survived the attack on Pearl Harbor:

_____

1.48   Event that ended isolationism and brought America into World War II:

_____

1.49   Number of Americans killed at Pearl Harbor: _____ .

Review the material in this section to prepare for the Self Test. The Self Test will check your understanding of this section. Any items you miss on this test will show you what areas you will need to restudy in order to prepare for the unit test.

SELF TEST 1

Match these people. Some will be used more than once (each answer, 2 points).

1.01 _____ dictator of Italy

1.02 _____ prime minister of Great Britain

1.03 _____ Communist dictator of the Soviet Union

1.04 _____ dictator of Germany

1.05 _____ invaded Ethiopia in 1935

1.06 _____ hated Jews, believed his people were a master race

1.07 _____ head of the Nazi Party

1.08 _____ elected president of the U.S. four times

1.09 _____ president blamed for the Great Depression

1.010 _____ president at the start of World War II

a. Franklin D. Roosevelt

b. Herbert Hoover

c. Benito Mussolini

d. Adolf Hitler

e. Winston Churchill

f. Joseph Stalin

Choose the correct item from the list (each answer, 3 points).

Tennessee Valley Authority	bank holiday	Bonus Army	Dust Bowl
Civilian Conservation Corp	Hundred Days	World War II	New Deal
Good Neighbor Policy			Lend-Lease

1.011 FDR's program to end the Great Depression: _____

1.012 Roosevelt's first action as president: _____

1.013 Event that ended the Great Depression: _____

1.014 Veterans that marched on Washington to get money they were promised for serving in World War I: _____

1.015 FDR began to treat the nations of our hemisphere as equals:

_____

1.016 Provided jobs and electricity in one of the poorest parts of the nation:

_____

1.017   Plan to give the Allies all the war supplies they needed to win the war:

_____

1.018   Drought in the Great Plains during the Great Depression: _____

1.019   The first part of FDR's term as president when many laws were passed:

_____

1.020   Popular public works program for young men in the Great Depression:

_____

Give the information requested (each answer, 3 points).

1.021   Event that started World War II: _____

1.022   At the worst part of the Great Depression, the fraction of workers without jobs:

_____

1.023   World organization that could not stop aggression before World War II:

_____

1.024   Nazi symbol, stands for hatred today: _____

1.025   European nation that refused to surrender to Germany in 1940–41:

_____

1.026   Name for the alliance of Germany, Italy, and Japan:

_____

1.027   Germany made a treaty with this nation to divide Poland in 1939, then invaded it

anyway in 1941: _____

1.028   Event that ended American isolationism and got the nation into World War II:

_____

1.029   The peace goals of Winston Churchill and Franklin Roosevelt:

_____

1.030   Britain and France appeased Hitler by giving him land in this country at the Munich

Conference of 1938: _____

Answer *true* or *false* (each answer, 2 points).

1.031 _____ Thousands of Americans wandered around the country looking for work during the Great Depression.

1.032 _____ Before the Great Depression, the U.S. government had never tried to use its money to feed people, create jobs, and help businesses.

1.033 _____ Franklin Roosevelt was allowed by Congress to pack the Supreme Court with new judges that agreed with his policies.

1.034 _____ Japan conquered Manchuria before World War II.

1.035 _____ Britain and France opposed German expansion by force from the time it began in the 1930s.

1.036 _____ Vichy France was the name France used for the part of Germany they occupied before World War II.

1.037 _____ Germany used trench warfare again in World War II.

1.038 _____ The Netherlands, Norway, Belgium, and Greece were all conquered by Germany in World War II.

1.039 _____ Most Americans realized that Germany and her allies were a threat to the United States and wanted to help the Allies.

1.040 _____ The *USS Arizona* was sunk by a German U-boat near Canada, killing most of the crew.

Teacher check:

Score _____

Initials _____

Date _____

80 / 100

2. THE WAR IN EUROPE

When the U.S. declared war on Japan, Germany declared war on America. Because the situation in Europe was so desperate, FDR agreed to take care of Hitler first, then Japan. That does not mean that nothing was done in the Pacific. It is just that most of the supplies and effort were focused on Europe at first.

America began immediately sending soldiers and supplies to Britain preparing for an attack on "Fortress Europe." The Allies had to prepare for *amphibious assaults*, attacks from the sea onto land. They attacked first in North Africa, then Italy, and finally in 1944 in France, while the Soviets were fighting in the east. It took four years to defeat Hitler.

Objectives

Review these objectives. When you have completed this section, you should be able to:

3. Describe World War II: especially its beginning, turning point, and events that led to the end of the war.
4. Describe American participation and strategy in World War II.
5. Name the leaders of World War II.

Vocabulary

Study these new words. Learning the meanings of these words is a good study habit and will improve your understanding of this LIFEPAC.

code (kōd). An arrangement of words or figures to keep a message short or secret; system of secret writing.

liberate (lib' ə rāt). To set free.

prejudice (prej' ə dis). An opinion formed without taking time and care to judge fairly.

ration (rash' ən or rā' shən). To allow only certain amounts to people; to distribute in limited amounts.

rivet (riv' it). A metal bolt with a head at one end; the end opposite the head is hammered to form another head after it is passed through the things to be joined; rivets are often used to fasten heavy steel beams together.

sabotage (sab' ə täzh). Damage done purposely to property, usually by enemy agents.

weld (weld). To join pieces of metal or plastic together by bringing the parts that touch to the melting point, so that they flow together and become one piece in cooling.

Note: *All vocabulary words in this LIFEPAC appear in* **boldface** *print the first time they are used. If you are unsure of the meaning when you are reading, study the definitions given.*

Pronunciation Key: hat, āge, cãre, fär; let, ēqual, tėrm; it, īce; hot, ōpen, ôrder; oil; out; cup, pùt, rüle; child; long; thin; /ŦH/ for then; /zh/ for measure; /u/ or /ə/ represents /a/ in about, /e/ in taken, /i/ in pencil, /o/ in lemon, and /u/ in circus.

The Home Front

Ideas. World War II was not a crusade to end all wars like World War I. The Allies were fighting for survival, not ideals. The Axis powers controlled almost all of Europe and much of the Far East in 1942. However, the unity in America was astounding. Never before in any war had the nation been so completely committed to the fight. All of America was willing to pay whatever price was needed to destroy the dictators who had been responsible for Pearl Harbor. Every American believed they were a part of the fight. Some went to fight on the fronts of Europe and Asia. Others stayed in the U.S. and fought at what was called the "home front."

| "Rosy the Riveter" was a symbol of women in the factories.

Production. The Great Depression ended shortly after Pearl Harbor. The American army needed tanks, guns, uniforms, food, backpacks, and hundreds of other things to go to war. Soon, everyone who wanted a job had one. Fifteen million Americans joined the armed services (army, navy, and air force). That meant there were fewer men to work in the factories. So, thousands of women went to work for the first time. They worked at all kinds of jobs, even the jobs that had always been held by men like **welding** and putting **rivets** into airplanes.

It was astounding what America was able to produce during the war. The big car manufacturers like Chrysler and Ford stopped making cars. Instead they made tanks, airplanes, jeeps, and artillery. Aircraft carriers that used to take 3 years to build were built in just over one year. Cargo ships that used to take a year to build were built in two months. One shipyard even managed to build and launch a cargo ship in about 4 days! By 1943, the U.S. was building twice as many weapons as all of the Axis nations put together! This huge river of goods was a key part of the flood that destroyed the Axis Powers.

Americans also had to produce much of the food to feed the Allies, as they had in World War I. In spite of the fact that so many men were gone to war, food production rose quickly. Americans helped out by growing their own vegetables in "victory gardens." These small gardens were planted everywhere, even in empty lots in the cities.

Life at Home. America was never attacked during the war, except at Pearl Harbor and a few of the Aleutian Islands in Alaska. Our nation was spared the destruction of war and bombing. However, the war did change life in America.

Goods for people were hard to find because most of the factories were making army boots, not shoes, for example. Many things during the war were **rationed**. Every month each household would get a book of ration cards that would allow them a certain amount of meat, sugar, shoes, butter, gasoline, and other hard-to-find goods. When the ration cards for meat were gone, the family could not buy any more meat that month, even if they had the money for it.

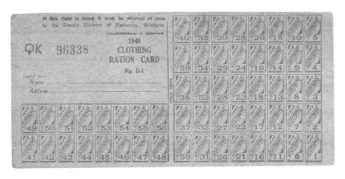

| A clothing ration card

Americans also tried to recycle and save things to help the war effort. Factories needed metal to make weapons, so Americans went on a giant scrap hunt. Old radiators in abandoned homes, old metal beds in the attic and broken buckets in the basement were gathered up and sent in to be recycled. Everyone made do with less. Girls shared their roller skates. Boys played with homemade toys. Mothers patched clothes rather than buying new ones. Everyone did all they could with only one goal in mind—victory.

Japanese Internment. The people of the United States were angry and scared after the attack on Pearl Harbor. The people of the west coast were afraid the Japanese navy would attack there next. Acting on fear and **prejudice**, they interned (imprisoned) the Japanese-Americans living on the West Coast.

President Roosevelt ordered the Japanese to move to internment camps away from the coast. The official reason was the government was afraid they would help with a Japanese invasion by committing **sabotage**. Most of the people who were moved were American citizens, the children of Japanese immigrants. They lost their homes and jobs. Many of the young men still volunteered for the army and served bravely, fighting for the nation that did not trust them.

| Housing at Manzanar internment camp

Battle of the Atlantic. One of the most important battles of World War II was the fight for control of the Atlantic Ocean. If the Allies were going to win the war, they had to get men and supplies to Great Britain and the Soviet Union. The people of Great Britain, for example, would have starved without American food. The Germans were trying to stop the ships carrying these cargoes the same way they had in World War I, by using submarines.

The battle between the Allied navies and the German submarines was called the "Battle of the Atlantic." Great Britain's large navy had stopped the German surface ships by late 1941; that left only the submarines. The subs hunted for Allied cargo ships in groups called "wolf packs." They were very effective. The U.S. lost hundreds of ships, their men, and valuable cargoes in the early part of the war.

However, the Allies fought back. They set up convoys, as they had in World War I. They used both navy warships and airplanes to chase and attack the German submarines. They also were able to use the newly invented *sonar*, which could find the subs underwater. By 1943 the Allies were destroying the German subs faster than Hitler could replace them.

The Allies also won the Battle of the Atlantic by sheer numbers. The Americans just kept the supply of men and goods coming at all costs.

| German U-boats torpedoed supply ships.

The great American factories made more ships and goods faster and faster. The Germans could not stop all of them. By 1943 the U.S. was building ships faster than the Germans could sink them. The result was that Britain and the Soviet Union got their supplies, the American army was moved to Europe to begin the attack on Hitler, and the Battle of the Atlantic was a resounding American victory.

Answer these questions.

2.1   How many Americans joined the armed services? _____

2.2   The "fighting" to produce goods in America was called which front?

_____

2.3   What was so important about American production during World War II?

_____

_____

_____

2.4   What was the name of the battle that was fought to stop German submarines from

sinking Allied ships going to Europe? _____

2.5   Americans helped grow food by planting what? _____

2.6   Groups of Nazi submarines were called what? _____

2.7   America was attacked in what two places during the war?

_____

2.8   How did the Allies win the Battle of the Atlantic? _____

_____

2.9   What was the attitude of most Americans after Pearl Harbor?

_____

_____

2.10   What happened to the Japanese people living on the west coast of America?

_____

_____

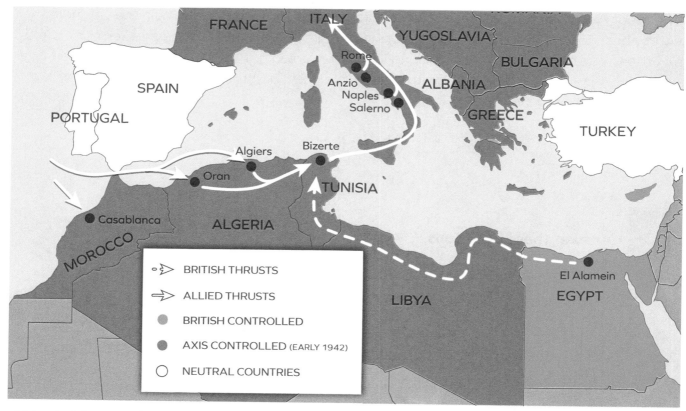

| North Africa and Italian Campaign

Turning Point

Hitler's big mistake. America's first full year of war (1942) was when things began to improve for the Allies. However, the first part of the year looked bad, especially in Asia. Japan had incredible successes early in 1942. The Japanese military captured Hong Kong, Thailand, Guam, Wake Island, the Philippines, the East Indies (the islands between Asia and Australia), and part of the island of New Guinea just north of Australia. It looked as if nothing could stop the Japanese victories.

The situation was a little different in Europe because Hitler made a very serious mistake. He attacked the Soviet Union in June of 1941. He expected to conquer it in a few weeks. That was his mistake. He was so confident that he was only prepared for summer fighting.

The Soviet people fought bravely once they realized that Hitler was a worse enemy than their own communist dictators. They retreated in front of the Nazi army, destroying everything useful: buildings, bridges, roads, and crops. They fought to slow the Germans. The Soviet commander was waiting for the arrival of his country's best fighter, "General Winter."

| White clothing and helmets helped the Russians to blend into the snow.

HISTORY & GEOGRAPHY 507

LIFEPAC TEST

NAME _____

DATE _____

SCORE _____

HISTORY & GEOGRAPHY 507: LIFEPAC TEST

Match these people (each answer, 2 points).

1. _____ prime minister of Great Britain

2. _____ losing U.S. commander in the Philippines; winner in New Guinea; military governor of Japan

3. _____ successful U.S. field general; slapped two soldiers

4. _____ British general

5. _____ Soviet dictator

6. _____ U.S. president who decided to use the atomic bomb on Japan

7. _____ U.S. president blamed for the Great Depression

8. _____ German dictator

9. _____ U.S. president at the beginning of World War II; New Deal

10. _____ supreme Allied commander for the major invasions of Europe; U.S. general

a. Harry S. Truman

b. Adolf Hitler

c. Winston Churchill

d. Douglas MacArthur

e. Franklin D. Roosevelt

f. Dwight D. Eisenhower

g. Joseph Stalin

h. George Patton

i. Bernard Montgomery

j. Herbert Hoover

Give the information requested (each numbered question, 3 points).

11. The American strategy in the Pacific was called _____ .

12. World War II began when Germany invaded _____ .

13. World War II ended when the U.S. dropped _____ on Hiroshima and Nagasaki.

14. The U.S. got into World War II when _____ attacked _____ _____ .

15. The Great Depression ended when _____ began.

16. At the worst of the Great Depression, _____ out of _____ people were out of work.

17. The turning point of the war in the Pacific was at the battle for _____ Island.

18. The big mistake made by Nazi Germany's leader during World War II was to invade _____ without preparing for winter fighting.

19. On D-Day the Allies invaded _____ .

20. The American project to build an atomic bomb was called the _____ Project.

21. First naval battle in history in which the ships did not see each other was at the Battle of the _____ Sea.

22. The murder of millions of innocent people, especially Jews, in Nazi Germany was called the _____ .

23. The turning point of the war in Europe was at the battle for the city of _____ .

24. The first place invaded by the Americans in the war in Europe (Operation Torch) was _____ .

25. The American bombing attack on Tokyo by bombers that took off from aircraft carriers and crashed in China was called _____ Raid.

26. The popular public works program for young men that planted trees and built roads during the Great Depression was called the _____ _____ .

27. The U.S. plan to give the Allies what they needed to win the war, even when the U.S. was still neutral was called _____ .

28. The Axis nation that tried to surrender when it was first invaded, but Germany prevented it, was _____ .

29. The association of nations created after World War II is called _____ _____ .

30. The association of nations that could not stop aggression before World War II was the _____ of _____ .

Answer *true* or *false* (each answer, 2 points).

31. _____ The American home front helped a lot in winning World War II by producing goods and supplies quickly.

32. _____ The fight to get supplies to Europe past the German submarines was called the Transport Battle.

33. _____ The U.S. was able to defend the Philippines against the Japanese for the whole war.

34. _____ Germany and the Soviet Union made a treaty in 1939 and agreed to divide Poland between themselves.

35. _____ France was conquered and most of it occupied by Germany in World War II.

36. _____ The Dust Bowl was the German attack on Great Britain.

37. _____ Much of the British army was rescued from France by hundreds of boats at Calais.

38. _____ German warfare in World War II was *blitzkrieg*, which used speed and surprise.

39. _____ Japanese soldiers fought to the death on the Pacific islands.

40. _____ Nothing was done to punish the leaders of Nazi Germany.

The winter of 1941–42 was one of the worst in many years in the Soviet Union. The Soviet army was ready for it with special equipment and warm, white clothes that made them hard to see in the snow. Thanks to Hitler's mistake, however, the Germans were not ready. Their weapons, tanks, and trucks would not work. Their men froze because they had no heavy winter clothes. General Winter stopped Hitler.

The Nazis won some victories in 1942, but they were stopped for good the next winter at Stalingrad (now called Volgograd). The Nazis and the Soviets fought over the city for about five months. The Nazis fought their way into the city house by house, and the Soviets drove them out the same way. An entire German army was finally trapped and captured in the city in January of 1943. That was the turning point of the war in Europe.

North Africa. The communist dictator, Joseph Stalin, had made a treaty with Hitler in 1939 before Hitler invaded his country in 1941. Stalin was a brutal man who did not trust anyone, least of all his new allies, Great Britain and the United States. He insisted that the democracies had to open a new front in Europe at once. His Soviet army was the only one fighting Hitler in Europe in 1941. FDR and Churchill understood why he wanted help; however, they did not have enough men and amphibious landing boats to attack France from Britain before 1944.

However, to give Stalin some help, they decided to attack North Africa in 1942. The invasion was **code**-named "Torch." Much of that region was under Axis control, and it was not as heavily defended as Europe. Also, the British still held Egypt. The British could come from there while the Americans attacked from the west. Then, once the Allies controlled North Africa, they could attack Europe from the south. (The invasion of North Africa, therefore, was still considered part of the war in Europe.)

General Dwight David Eisenhower, one of America's heroes in the war, was put in command of Operation Torch. He would go on to also be the supreme Allied commander in Europe for the invasions of Italy and France. He was good with people. He was able to get all of the proud British, French, and other Allied commanders to work together. It was not an easy job.

The British army won its first victory of the war in October of 1942 when it defeated the Germans at El Alamein in Egypt. In November 1942, Eisenhower's forces landed in Morocco, putting the Germans in between the two Allied armies.

| General Dwight D. Eisenhower

The Vichy French government (which controlled Morocco) fought the Allies at first because they had surrendered to Germany already. However, the French wanted to free their homeland from the Germans, not fight the Allies. They quickly changed sides, fighting with the Allies as the Free French, under the command of Charles de Gaulle, a French general who had refused to surrender to the Germans.

The two Allied armies fought from both ends of North Africa, forcing the Germans into a smaller and smaller piece of land in the center. The German commander, Erwin Rommel (called "the Desert Fox") fought hard, but the Allies could not be stopped. The last Nazi forces in North Africa were captured in May of 1943. Now, the Allies had a base which they could use to attack Europe to the north.

Italy. Italy had not been doing well in the war. Germany had to help the Italians take Greece in 1941, and the Italians felt they were not being treated as equals by Hitler. The Allies hoped they could get Italy to surrender by attacking it from North Africa, so the Allies decided to invade Italy in July of 1943, starting in Sicily.

The invasion of Sicily, the big island south of the Italian Peninsula, was led by British General Bernard Montgomery and American General George Patton. Montgomery was one of Britain's greatest heroes of the war. He was the man who won at El Alamein in Egypt. Patton was a great American hero who had been a key field general in the invasion of North Africa. However, he was a man who also got himself into problems when he was not fighting. He was an arrogant man who loved war. He got in trouble for slapping two soldiers in a hospital because he believed they were faking their illnesses. However, he was a very successful general in the field.

| Bernard Montgomery

Sicily was captured in about a month. The Italian people were tired of the war. When Sicily was attacked, they overthrew their dictator, Mussolini, and tried to surrender. However, Hitler would not allow the Italians to give up. The Nazi army invaded Italy, put Mussolini back in power, and forced the Italian army to keep fighting. The Nazis fought off the Allies themselves. The German army fought hard all the way up the Italian Peninsula. Italy did not actually surrender until May of 1945, just before Germany surrendered.

Complete these sentences.

2.11 In Europe, the Allies invaded _____ first and then
_____ after America joined the war.

2.12 The turning point of the war in Europe was the battle for the city of
_____ in the Soviet Union.

2.13 The Allied commander on Operation Torch was _____
_____ .

2.14 The generals who led the invasion of Sicily were _____
and _____ .

2.15 Britain's first victory of the war was under the command of General
_____ at _____ in Egypt.

2.16 The leader of the Free French was _____ .

2.17 The German commander in North Africa was _____ .

2.18 Hitler's big mistake was to invade _____ without preparing
to fight in the _____ .

2.19 Italy overthrew Mussolini and tried to surrender when the Allies invaded _____ .

2.20 Italy was forced to keep fighting by the _____ .

2.21 Morocco was controlled by _____ when the Allies invaded.

2.22 Sicily was conquered in about _____ after it was invaded.

2.23 The communist dictator of the Soviet Union who wanted the Allies to invade Europe
was _____ .

2.24 Italy finally surrendered for real in _____ of _____ .

D-Day

Normandy. The Germans knew that the Allies were planning to invade France from Great Britain. The U.S. had been building up a huge supply of food, tanks, guns, ammunition, bombs, and trucks in England for the invasion. They could not hide all of that. The Germans were also expecting the invasion to come early in the summer of 1944; but they did not know where it would be, and they had to protect 3,000 miles of coastline in Europe. Calais was the closest land in France to Britain. That is where the Germans expected the invasion. However, that is not what the Allies were planning. They were planning instead to invade France at Normandy, miles west of Calais, hoping to catch the Germans by surprise.

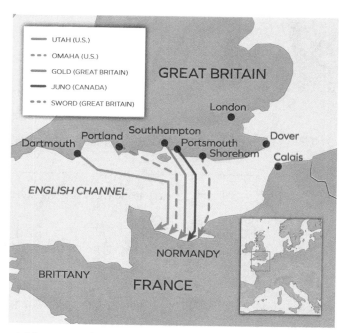

| Normandy invasion plan

The invasion of Normandy was code named "Overlord." The day the invasion was to take place was called "D-Day." It was a very important invasion. If the Germans could stop the Allies from landing on the beaches of Normandy or stop them from advancing, they would have no choice but to return to England. It would be months, if not another year, before another invasion could be attempted. The Soviet Union might collapse or make peace in that time, leaving Britain and America to fight Hitler by themselves.

D-Day. Eisenhower finally decided to invade Normandy on June 6, 1944. Over 150,000 men crossed the English Channel on the night of June 5th. They came in over a thousand ships, with 10,000 airplanes protecting them and 1,500 tanks ready to move into France. The weather was not very good, so the Germans were not expecting the attack that day.

| Much of the Normandy beaches were cluttered with barbed wire.

| German obstacles on the beach stopped the landing craft from getting up on the beach, and soldiers had to wade through the water to get to the beach.

Five Allied armies landed at five beaches in Normandy at dawn on D-Day. They used over four thousand landing boats that could float up close to land, drop a gate in the front, and allow the men to land in shallow water. The Americans attacked the beaches code named "Utah" and "Omaha" in the west. The British attacked "Gold" in the center. East of them, the Canadians attacked "Juno" and the British attacked "Sword."

The worst fighting was at Omaha. High cliffs above the beach allowed the Germans to fire down on the Americans. This also made it difficult for the invaders to move off of the beach once they landed. As many as nine out of ten of the first groups of Americans ashore were killed or wounded. Twenty-four hundred Americans were killed or wounded on that one beach that day.

The invasion, however, was a success. By the end of the day, the armies were safely on land and moving off the beaches, even at Omaha. The stiff German fighting, however, kept the Allies confined in Normandy for over a month. It was not until July that the Allies broke through the German lines and began to move into France.

The end of Nazi Germany. Once the Allied armies could get into France with all of their strength, Germany was doomed. The Soviet army had been steadily pushing the Germans back since Stalingrad, so Germany was trapped between two advancing armies. Paris was **liberated** in August of 1944 after four years of Nazi occupation. General Patton's tank army moved forward toward the German border so quickly that he used up all of his supplies of gasoline and had to stop to get more. The British moved in to free Belgium

| The German Reichstag after its capture by soviet troops (edifice in Berlin, Germany)

in September. Because winter was coming, the final attack on Germany did not come until the early months of 1945. Hitler tried to stop the Allies at the Battle of the Bulge in December 1944, but he failed.

The Soviet Union came in from the east, taking Warsaw, the capital of Poland, in January of 1945 and in February took Vienna, the capital of Austria. Then, the Soviet army moved into Germany. The British and Canadian armies came into Germany through the Netherlands to the north. The Americans came straight in from France to the west. The Soviet troops surrounded the German capital, Berlin, in April of 1945. Once they captured it, the Soviets destroyed the city. Hitler committed suicide on April 30, and Germany surrendered on May 7, 1945. That day was called V-E Day, Victory in Europe Day.

Holocaust

As the Allied armies moved into Germany they discovered just how horrible Hitler truly was. Hitler had hated all races except the Germans, and he tried to destroy many of them. The Allies found concentration camps where Jews, Slavs, Gypsies, and people who spoke against Hitler had been imprisoned. The people who were alive were little more than walking skeletons, having been worked almost to death. Many others had not survived, and thousands of bodies were found.

The Jews had taken the worst of Hitler's vile hatred. Many of them had been shipped to death camps where the old, the weak, and the children were killed by poison gas. The young and strong were put to work for as long as they could survive. Approximately six million European Jews and as many as four million other people were killed in Nazi Germany (that does not include those who died in the war). This Nazi mass murder was named the *Holocaust*.

The horror of the Holocaust made the Allies decide to bring the leaders of Nazi Germany to trial. Several of them were condemned to die for "crimes against humanity" at a special court held in Nuremberg, Germany in 1945 and 1946. Others received long terms in prison. This was unusual because defeated commanders in a war are usually not put in prison. However, the deaths of so many innocent people by murder and working them to death just could not be ignored.

| Auschwitz extermination camp where people were worked to death and executed by poison gas.

Give the information requested.

2.25   Name for the day France was invaded by the Allies: _____

2.26   The code names for the American beaches at Normandy:

_____

2.27   The invasion of Normandy's code name: _____

2.28   The name given to Hitler's murder of millions of innocent people:

_____

2.29   May 7, 1945 was this day: _____

2.30   Where the Germans expected the invasion of France: _____

2.31   When Paris was liberated: _____

2.32   American general who went so fast he ran out of gas:

_____

2.33   Date of the invasion of Normandy: _____

2.34   What Hitler did to avoid being captured: _____

2.35   Place where Nazi leaders were tried for crimes against humanity:

_____

2.36   Army that captured Berlin: _____

2.37   The beach that had the worst fighting at Normandy:

_____

2.38   Battle in December 1944 when Hitler tried to stop the Allies:

_____

2.39   Number of Jews believed killed in Nazi Germany:

_____

Review the material in this section to prepare for the Self Test. The Self Test will check your understanding of this section and the previous section. Any items you miss on this test will show you what areas you will need to restudy in order to prepare for the unit test.

SELF TEST 2

Match these people (each answer, 2 points).

2.01 _____ dictator of Italy

2.02 _____ British general

2.03 _____ American general; commanded the Allied invasions; good with people

2.04 _____ German dictator

2.05 _____ president blamed for the Great Depression

2.06 _____ leader of the Free French

2.07 _____ Communist dictator of the Soviet Union

2.08 _____ president at the beginning of World War II

2.09 _____ American general; good field commander; got in trouble for slapping sick soldiers

2.010 _____ British prime minister

a. Herbert Hoover

b. Franklin Roosevelt

c. Adolf Hitler

d. Winston Churchill

e. Joseph Stalin

f. Dwight Eisenhower

g. George Patton

h. Charles de Gaulle

i. Benito Mussolini

j. Bernard Montgomery

Name the person, place, battle, or item (each answer, 3 points).

2.011 _____ Place in France invaded on D-Day, June 6, 1944

2.012 _____ FDR's program to end the Great Depression

2.013 _____ Part of France that was not occupied by Germany

2.014 _____ Attack that brought the U.S. into the war

2.015 _____ Hitler's murder of millions of innocent people

2.016 _____ The first part of FDR's presidency when many laws were passed to fight the Great Depression

2.017 _____ Event that ended the Great Depression

2.018 _____ Event that started World War II in 1939

2.019 _____ The battle against the German submarines trying to sink Allied ships going to Europe

2.020 _____ Alliance of Germany, Italy, and Japan

Choose the correct letter to complete each sentence (each answer, 3 points).

2.021 The _____ people on the west coast of the U.S. were interned.

    a. German   b. Chinese   c. Italian   d. Japanese

2.022 Hitler's big mistake in World War II was _____ .

    a. invading Poland without his tanks

    b. invading the Soviet Union without preparing for winter fighting

    c. killing the Jews whom he needed to run German factories

    d. expecting that the U.S. would never fight in Europe

2.023 The Allies began to retake Europe by invading, in order, _____ .

    a. France, Sicily, and North Africa   b. North Africa, Italy, and France

    c. Russia, Austria, and Italy   d. Normandy, Berlin, and Greece

2.024 The turning point of the war in Europe was at _____ .

    a. Stalingrad   b. the Battle of the Bulge

    c. Normandy   d. Pearl Harbor

2.025 The first British victory was at _____ .

    a. Normandy   b. the Battle of the Bulge

    c. El Alamein   d. Sicily

2.026 After the invasion of Sicily, Italy _____ .

    a. fought to the last man   b. tried to surrender

    c. joined the Allies   d. drove the Allies off the island

2.027 The worst fighting during the D-Day invasion was at the American beach code named _____ .

    a. Utah   b. Sword   c. Juno   d. Omaha

2.028 Adolf Hitler _____ .

    a. was captured by the French and hanged

    b. committed suicide before Germany surrendered

    c. was shot in battle by the Soviet army

    d. disappeared without a trace at the end of the war

2.029   The one European nation that continued to fight Germany after France was defeated in 1940 was _____ .

    a. the Netherlands b. Austria   c. Greece   d. Great Britain

2.030   The American program to give the Allies what they needed to win the war was called _____ .

    a. the Good Neighbor Policy   b. Lend-Lease

    c. the New Deal   d. Rationing

Answer *true* or *false* (each answer, 2 points).

2.031   _____ The home front was the fighting with German soldiers in America.

2.032   _____ American productions of goods had little to do with winning World War II.

2.033   _____ Hitler and Stalin signed a treaty in 1939 and agreed to divide Poland.

2.034   _____ Germany was defeated when the nation and its armies were trapped between the Soviet army in the east and the other Allied forces in the west.

2.035   _____ After World War II, some of the Nazi leaders were condemned to die for crimes against humanity.

2.036   _____ Americans fought in World War II for the same ideals they fought for in World War I.

2.037   _____ At the worst part of the Great Depression, one out of four people did not have jobs.

2.038   _____ The League of Nations was not able to control aggression by the dictators before World War II.

2.039   _____ The Atlantic Charter was the British-American plan to defeat Japan.

2.040   _____ Germany never defeated the Netherlands or Norway.

Teacher check:

Score _____

Initials _____

Date _____

80 / 100

3. THE WAR IN THE PACIFIC

While the Allies were fighting in Europe, they still had to worry about Asia. Most of the fighting there was done by the Americans. The Soviet Union did not even go to war with Japan until after V-E Day. The British had some forces in Asia, as did Australia, which was directly threatened by Japan, but it was the American navy that stopped the Japanese advance. It was the American navy, army, and marines that began slowly hopping from one island to another back toward the Japanese home islands. It was the U.S. that finally ended the war by using the newly invented atomic bomb on two Japanese cities.

Objectives

Review these objectives. When you have completed this section, you should be able to:

3. Describe World War II: especially its beginning, turning point, and events that led up to the end of the war.
4. Describe American participation and strategy in World War II.
5. Name the leaders of World War II.

Vocabulary

Study these new words. Learning the meanings of these words is a good study habit and will improve your understanding of this LIFEPAC.

abortion (ə bȯr′ shən). A medical procedure to kill a baby before it is born.

radiation (rā′ dē ā′ shən). The rays or tiny particles that are given off by the atoms of a radioactive substance; radioactivity (This can be harmful to living tissue.).

refugee (ref′ yə jē′). A person who flees from his home, often to another country, for safety from war or persecution.

volcanic (vol kan′ ik). Of or caused by a volcano; having to do with volcanoes.

Pronunciation Key: hat, āge, cãre, fär; let, ēqual, tėrm; it, īce; hot, ōpen, ôrder; oil; out; cup, pu̇t, rüle; child; long; thin; /ᵺH/ for then; /zh/ for measure; /u/ or /ə/ represents /a/ in about, /e/ in taken, /i/ in pencil, /o/ in lemon, and /u/ in circus.

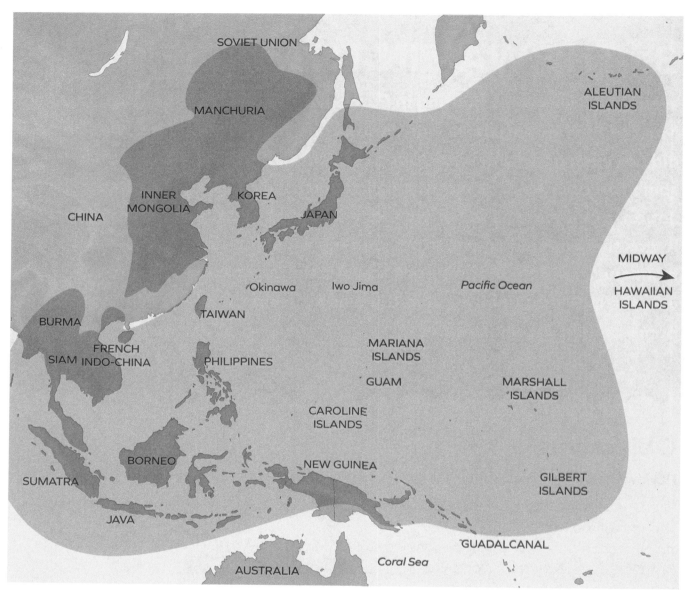

| The furthest extent of the Japanese Empire during World War II

Pacific Turning Point

Japanese victories. Like their Nazi allies, the Japanese won tremendous victories early in the war. After Pearl Harbor on December 7, 1941, Japan launched successful attacks all over southeast Asia. The British colony of Hong Kong and the American islands of Wake and Guam were taken in December. Thailand fell within hours. From Thailand, the Japanese army moved into the Malay Peninsula, capturing the British city of Singapore in February of 1942. The oil rich islands south of the peninsula fell the next month. To the north, the Japanese moved into Burma and were threatening India. They also cut off the Burma Road, the main route used to get supplies to the Chinese still fighting the Japanese army in their homeland.

The only place the Japanese faced serious fighting was in the American colony in the Philippines. The Philippines were attacked a few days after Pearl Harbor. The American army there was under the command of General Douglas MacArthur. The Americans retreated to a peninsula called Bataan at the mouth of Manila Bay. At the southern end of the peninsula was an island fortress called Corregidor.

The Americans fought bravely, but they did not have enough food. There was no way for the U.S. navy to bring them new supplies with the Japanese navy protecting the islands. The Americans held out until April on the peninsula and until May on Corregidor, but they were forced to surrender because they were so weak from lack of food. The Japanese cruelly forced their prisoners to march for miles to prison camps. It was called the "Bataan Death March." The men who collapsed on the way were killed.

MacArthur was ordered to leave before the army surrendered because FDR wanted to have him to lead the army in the Pacific. He left, as he was ordered, but promised, "I shall return." Thus, the Japanese Empire reached its largest size by the summer of 1942, leaving the Allies with nothing except a string of losses.

| General Douglas MacArthur (center) marching ashore in the Philippines

| Corregidor ruins

Problems for Japan. The American fleet in the Pacific was very weak after Pearl Harbor. The main survivors of the attack were the aircraft carriers. These were huge floating air fields. They were used to carry airplanes into battles on islands and coastlines. Most of America's fighting in 1942 was done by airplanes off of these carriers.

Americans wanted to punish Japan after the sneak attack on Pearl Harbor. In 1942 Lieutenant Colonel Jimmy Doolittle led a daring raid to do just that. Big bombing planes called B-25's were changed so they could take off from an aircraft carrier. Sixteen of these bombers took off from the carrier Hornet in April and bombed Tokyo, the capital of Japan. The planes had no safe place to land, so they crash landed in China. The Chinese people got most of the pilots home safely. It was called "Doolittle's Raid." It did not hurt Japan much, but it was a big boost for the Americans, who had only seen Japanese victories in the Pacific up until then.

| Aircraft carriers were floating airfields with long runways for airplanes.

Japan controlled the northern part of the island of New Guinea, just north of Australia, in 1942. In May they sent an invasion force by sea to attack Port Moresby, the Allied base on the south coast of the island. If they could take Port Moresby, the Japanese would be within easy reach of Australia. The invasion fleet was met by the U.S. navy at the Battle of the Coral Sea just east of New Guinea.

The Battle of the Coral Sea was a very unusual navy battle. It was the first navy battle in history in which the ships *never came within sight of each other*. It was fought completely by airplanes which came off the Japanese and American aircraft carriers to attack the enemy ships. Neither side clearly won the battle, but the Japanese retreated, leaving Port Moresby and Australia in Allied hands.

The U.S. suffered a serious loss in this battle, the aircraft carrier *Lexington*. It was hit and sank slowly. The American sailors very calmly abandoned ship, lining up their shoes on the edge of the deck before they left. Some of the men even filled their helmets with ice cream from the freezer to eat as they went. The other American ships picked up the men. The U.S. only had a few of these ships and would not be able to quickly replace the carrier that was lost.

Midway. Midway is a small American island about halfway between the U.S. and Asia. It was the next target of the Japanese navy. The Japanese fleet had four times as many ships as the Americans at Midway. They had four large aircraft carriers and three smaller ones in their large attack fleet. The Americans had only three large carriers plus about forty-five other ships, but because the Americans had broken a Japanese code, they knew their enemies were coming. The U.S. fleet laid a trap which the Japanese sailed into in June of 1942.

The Battle of Midway, like the Coral Sea, was fought by airplanes. The American planes caught the Japanese carriers while they were preparing their own planes to be launched. The decks of the Japanese ships were covered with parked planes, bombs, and fuel. All four of Japan's large aircraft carriers were sunk. They also lost 200 planes and their pilots. The Americans lost one aircraft carrier, the *Yorktown*, and 150 planes. It was a huge American victory.

Midway was the turning point of the war in the Pacific. The Japanese navy lost four out of its nine large aircraft carriers in one day. The attack fleet retreated back to safer waters. They would not win another important battle for the rest of the war.

| Battles with aircraft carriers were actually battles of airplanes against ships.

Complete these sentences.

3.1 The turning point of the war in the Pacific was at the Battle of _____ .

3.2 The Battle of the Coral Sea was the first navy battle in which the enemy ships

_____ .

3.3 American bombers hit Tokyo during _____ in April of 1942.

3.4 The U.S. lost the carrier _____ at the Coral Sea and the

_____ at Midway.

3.5 In the Philippines, the American army retreated to the _____

peninsula and the fortress island of _____ .

3.6 The Battles of the Coral Sea and Midway were fought by _____ .

3.7 American prisoners in the Philippines were killed when they collapsed walking to

prison camps during the _____ .

3.8   The Japanese army cut the _____ in 1942, the road used to supply China's army.

3.9   General _____ was ordered to leave the Philippines before the American army surrendered, but he promised to return.

3.10   Japan lost _____ large aircraft carriers at Midway.

3.11   The Americans knew the Japanese were attacking Midway because they had

_____ .

3.12   The Japanese were trying to invade _____ on the southern side of the island of _____ when the Battle of the Coral Sea took place.

Island Hopping

Strategy. The U.S. came up with a great strategy for conquering the Japanese Empire. It was called "island hopping" or "leapfrogging." The Empire was made up of thousands of islands in the South Pacific. Many of these islands were heavily fortified and filled with determined Japanese soldiers. The U.S. navy decided to skip (hop) these islands. Instead, the navy and the marines attacked less fortified islands. As the American navy gained control of the seas and the sky over the islands, the Japanese soldiers on the islands that were not attacked were cut off from their supplies and had no one to fight. The Americans simply bombed them and left them alone to sit out the war while their supplies ran low.

The plan worked very well. The U.S. airplanes would bomb an island first. Then, the marines would invade it. An airfield would be built on the newly captured island. From there, planes would bomb the next island, starting the process all over again. Each island "hop" brought the Americans closer and closer to Japan.

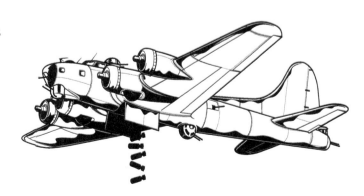

| Bombers would bomb an island first, before marines would invade.

First islands. The first island the Americans attacked was Guadalcanal in August of 1942. The island was at the southwest end of the Japanese Empire, just north of the Coral Sea. The Allies needed to capture a Japanese airfield on the island that was used to attack Allied ships bringing supplies to Australia. It took six months of hard fighting to take the island.

The Allies under the command of General Douglas MacArthur were also fighting for control of New Guinea in 1942. The Japanese controlled the northern part of the island, the Allies controlled the south. MacArthur began a hopping plan of his own to retake the island at the end of 1942. He had the army hop along the coast, capturing key places as they went. Each place that was captured was used as a starting point to attack the next spot. It worked very well, even though MacArthur had to work with limited supplies and men. Most of the army was still needed in Europe. Still, he was able to push the Japanese off the island by the middle of 1944.

Other islands. Island hopping was brutal warfare. The Japanese had very strict ideas about how to fight a war. They believed it was a disgrace to be captured, so they fought to the death and almost never surrendered, even when they clearly could not win. As a result, thousands and thousands of Japanese and Americans died on every island. The island of Tarawa in the Gilbert Islands was a good example. A thousand U.S. service men died taking the island, and only 17 out of the 20,000 Japanese soldiers surrendered. The rest had to be killed, one by one. This was true on *every island* the Americans attacked.

Island hopping seriously began in 1943. In November, the Americans attacked the Gilberts, the bottom corner of the Japanese Empire. Using the captured Gilbert Islands as a base, a few of the Marshall Islands were taken in January and February of 1944. The Americans then moved to the Marianas Islands, hopping over the strongholds in the Caroline Islands.

Near those islands, the Battle of the Philippine Sea took place in June 1944. The U.S. navy did incredible damage to the Japanese fleet, destroying three aircraft carriers and about 500 planes. The Allied victory left the Japanese navy very weak. Moreover, the Marianas Islands were close enough to Japan to allow American planes to begin bombing Japanese cities. They would do that until the end of the war.

MacArthur fulfilled his promise to return to the Philippines in October of 1944 when he hopped north from New Guinea. The last major naval battle of the war took place at Leyte Gulf. Japan gambled by sending most of what was left of their fleet to stop the U.S. invasion of the Philippines. The Japanese fleet was destroyed, and the U.S. recaptured the islands after months of hard fighting. The last of the Japanese soldiers did not surrender until the war ended.

| Japanese soldiers would fight to the death and rarely surrender.

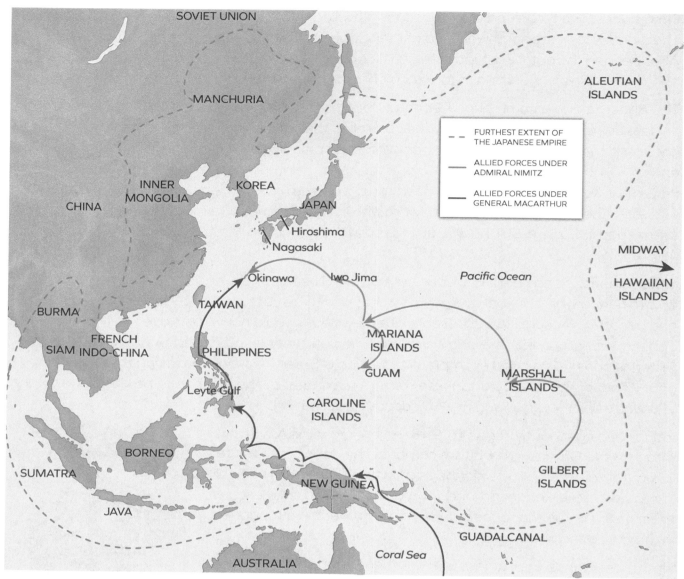

| "Island hopping" in the Pacific Ocean during World War II

The last islands. Two of the last islands that had to be taken, before conquering Japan, were among the most difficult to overcome. The first was Iwo Jima. The U.S. needed it for an airfield. It was so close to Japan that small fighter planes, which could not fly as far as the big bombers, could use it. They could fly with the bombers and protect them as they attacked the Japanese cities. Iwo Jima could also be used as an emergency landing place for the bombers when they were damaged and could not fly all the way back to the Marianas.

Iwo Jima was a **volcanic** island. It was covered with thousands of tiny caves. The Japanese soldiers hid in those caves and fought to the death. The U.S. Marine Corps remembers Iwo Jima because 7,000 of their soldiers died taking the island. Over 20,000 Japanese soldiers also died.

The second important island was Okinawa, just south of Japan. The U.S. needed it as a base to prepare for the invasion of Japan. It had been part of Japan for hundreds of years. The Japanese people thought of it as part of their nation, and the Americans knew they would defend it fiercely. They did. Over 100,000 Japanese soldiers and civilians died before the island was in U.S. hands in June.

After Germany surrendered in May of 1945, America was ready to focus all of her efforts on the invasion of Japan. There was little hope that the enemy would surrender. The Americans would have to fight their way up the Japanese islands, one by one. Hundreds of thousands, if not millions, of people were expected to die. Then, the U.S. found a dreadful alternative, the atomic bomb.

| The Iwo Jima Memorial in Washington D.C.

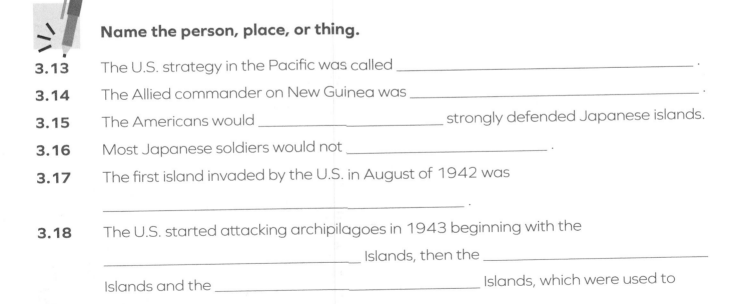

Name the person, place, or thing.

3.13 The U.S. strategy in the Pacific was called _____ .

3.14 The Allied commander on New Guinea was _____ .

3.15 The Americans would _____ strongly defended Japanese islands.

3.16 Most Japanese soldiers would not _____ .

3.17 The first island invaded by the U.S. in August of 1942 was

_____ .

3.18 The U.S. started attacking archipilagoes in 1943 beginning with the

_____ Islands, then the _____

Islands and the _____ Islands, which were used to

bomb Japan.

3.19   The U.S. Navy heavily damaged the Japanese fleet in June of 1944 at the Battle of

_____ .

3.20   The Japanese navy was destroyed at the Battle of _____
in October of 1944.

3.21   _____ marines died taking Iwo Jima.

3.22   In June of 1945, the U.S. captured _____ to use as a base
to invade Japan.

3.23   The U.S. did not believe _____ would surrender.

Final Victory

New President. Franklin D. Roosevelt ran for president again in 1944. He easily won re-election. Most people did not want to change leaders in the middle of a war, especially when things were going so well in November of 1944. However, FDR was old and growing weak. He died April 12, 1945, just after his fourth term started. He had been elected four times and had served as president for just over 12 years. No other president would ever equal that. Vice President Harry S. Truman became the nation's new leader for the last few months of the war.

Manhattan Project. Both Nazi Germany and the U.S. had been working hard to create a new weapon during the war. It was called the atomic bomb. It was a superbomb that could destroy most of a city by itself. The very secret U.S. program to create one was set up on a desert base in New Mexico. It was code named the "Manhattan Project."

The Manhattan Project secretly put hundreds of scientists together on the base. They lived there for much of the war. It was a small, hidden town that did not communicate much with the outside world. Children who were born there did not even have their birthplace written on their records. Only a few people out-side of the town even knew it existed.

| Harry S. Truman

The German project was stopped when they surrendered in May of 1945. However, the Americans scientists kept working. On July 16, 1945 the first atomic bomb exploded in the desert of New Mexico. President Truman was told about it at once.

Truman then had to make a very important decision. The atomic bomb could be used against Japan. It would destroy most of a city. Many of the people who survived the bomb would die later of burns and illnesses from the **radiation** the bomb made. It might be enough to convince Japan to surrender and save all the lives that would be lost in an invasion. Truman decided to use the bomb.

| An atomic bomb can destroy a city.

Hiroshima. A U.S. bomber named the *Enola Gay* carried the first atomic bomb to its target. The bomb was dropped on the Japanese city of Hiroshima on August 6, 1945. It went off above the center of the city creating a huge, mushroom-shaped cloud that rose high into the atmosphere. About five square miles of the city were completely destroyed. Buildings and people near "ground zero," where the bomb went off, were reduced to dust. As many as 100,000 people may have died that day from the bomb. Four times that many may have died later from the effects of the radiation.

Truman had warned Japan to surrender or be destroyed before he sent the bomb. Japan did not respond to that message, nor did it react after the first bomb fell. So, Truman ordered a second bomb (the only other one the U.S. had) dropped on the city of Nagasaki on August 9th. That was enough. Japan offered to surrender on August 10th.

The Japanese Empire surrendered on September 2, 1945 (V-J Day), ending World War II. The surrender ceremony took place on board the *USS Missouri*, which was part of the U.S. fleet in Tokyo Bay. Douglas MacArthur became the military governor of Japan. He helped the nation write a new constitution and rebuild as a democracy. The emperor kept his throne, but he no longer had any real power.

Results of the war. About seventeen million soldiers, Allied and Axis, died in World War II. The largest number of dead were in the Soviet Union where seven and a half million died. The United States lost 400,000 service men. As many as thirty-six million ordinary people also died. They were killed by bombs, starvation, and murder. When the war ended, millions of people in Europe and Japan were without homes. Millions of **refugees** moved around in Europe, trying to find a safe place to live. The U.S. was the only nation in good enough shape to help, and this time, unlike World War I, America did not return to isolationism.

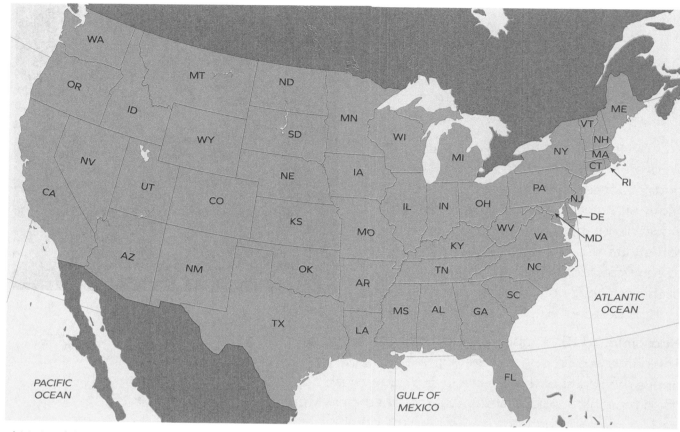

| United States in 1945

United Nations. The Atlantic Charter, written by Roosevelt and Winston Churchill in 1941, called for a new association of nations after the end of the war. The old League of Nations had proved worthless. The free nations wanted a place where they could meet, talk about problems, and take actions to protect the peace. This time the U.S. would support the effort. The result was the United Nations.

Delegates from fifty nations met in San Francisco, California in April of 1945, just days after FDR died. The important Allied nations (the U.S., Britain, and the Soviet Union) had already agreed on the main plan for the new organization. The delegates to the San Francisco Conference wrote a charter which explained the new organization's goals, powers, and methods of working. The new organization was named the United Nations.

| United Nations building in New York City

Its charter went into effect on October 24, 1945, a little over one month after the end of World War II. Its main office was built in New York City.

The United Nations would work better than the League of Nations because of the support it received from the rich democracies, especially the United States. The United Nations, U.N. for short, gives the nations of the world a safe place to talk about problems. Even nations that are at war or enemies will meet there. The U.N. also tries to help with world-wide problems like hunger and pollution. Moreover, the United States and other democracies have often obeyed the U.N. to stop trading with some nations and even send soldiers to fight them when they act aggressively. This has forced some warlike nations to stop what they were doing wrong.

The U.N. is far from a perfect organization. Its members often quarrel more than they cooperate. Decisions are too often based on hatred, not fairness. Many of the things the U.N. has decided are wrong to Christians, like encouraging **abortion**. Many Americans do not like the U.N. because they do not think other nations should make decisions for us. Still, the United States is a member and has worked with the U.N. on many good things since World War II. The U.S. was determined after World War II not to become isolationist again. The U.N. was part of the U.S. plan to make sure that there never would be a World War III.

| The U.N. flag; U.N. soldiers wear blue helmets and act as "peacekeepers" during conflicts.

Answer *true* or *false*.

3.24 _____ The Manhattan Project was the name of the U.S. program to build a new League of Nations.

3.25 _____ The U.S. and Nazi Germany were trying to build an atomic bomb.

3.26 _____ V-J Day was August 6, 1945.

3.27 _____ The surrender ceremony for Japan was held on the *USS Arizona* in Pearl Harbor.

3.28 _____ The first atomic bomb explosion happened in the desert of New Mexico on July 16, 1945.

3.29 _____ The first city destroyed by an atomic bomb was Tokyo.

3.30 _____ The United Nations charter was written by Great Britain, the U.S. and the Soviet Union at a meeting in the Atlantic Ocean near Canada.

3.31 _____ The atomic bomb at Hiroshima released radiation that killed more people than the explosion did.

3.32 _____ Truman decided to use the atomic bomb to avoid invading Japan.

3.33 _____ FDR was elected president three times and served 14 years as president.

3.34 _____ Harry S. Truman was elected president in 1944.

3.35 _____ The U.N.'s main office is in New York City.

3.36 _____ The U.N.'s charter went into effect on May 7, 1945.

3.37 _____ World War II ended when the U.S. dropped atomic bombs on two Japanese cities.

3.38 _____ America returned to isolationism again after World War II.

3.39 _____ Douglas MacArthur was the military governor of Germany after the war.

 Before you take this last Self Test, you may want to do one or more of these self checks.

1. _____ Read the objectives. See if you can do them.
2. _____ Restudy the material related to any objectives that you cannot do.
3. _____ Use the **SQ3R** study procedure to review the material:
    a. **S**can the sections.
    b. **Q**uestion yourself.
    c. **R**ead to answer your questions.
    d. **R**ecite the answers to yourself.
    e. **R**eview areas you did not understand.
4. _____ Review all vocabulary, activities, and Self Tests, writing a correct answer for every wrong answer.

SELF TEST 3

Complete the following (each answer, 4 points).

3.01   Describe the American strategy in the Pacific during World War II.

_____

_____

_____

3.02   What was the Manhattan Project?

_____

_____

_____

3.03   Describe what happened to the U.S. army in the Philippines after the Japanese invaded the island.

_____

_____

_____

3.04   What was unusual about the Battle of the Coral Sea?

_____

_____

_____

3.05   How did the Japanese soldiers fight on the Pacific islands?

_____

_____

_____

3.06   What got the U.S. into World War II?

_____

_____

_____

3.07   What happened on D-Day?

_____

_____

_____

3.08   What is the United Nations?

_____

_____

3.09   Describe Doolittle's Raid.

_____

_____

3.010   Why did the U.S. president decide to use the atomic bomb on Japan?

_____

_____

_____

Answer _true_ or _false_.

If the answer is _false_, change one or more of the underlined words to make it _true_ (each numbered question, 3 points). (Take off 1 point if the student correctly says the answer was false, but can not give the right correction.)

3.011   _____   <u>Charles</u> <u>de</u> <u>Gaulle</u> was the dictator of Italy.

3.012   _____   In the early part of the war, the Axis nations of Japan and <u>Great</u> <u>Britain</u> won large victories very quickly.

3.013   _____   <u>Midway</u> was the turning point for the war in the Pacific.

3.014   _____   <u>Franklin</u> <u>D</u>. <u>Roosevelt</u> was president when World War II ended.

3.015   _____   The first atomic bomb used in war was dropped on <u>Hiroshima</u>.

3.016   _____   The peace goals of Winston Churchill and FDR were written out in the <u>Atlantic</u> <u>Charter</u>.

3.017   _____   Adolf Hitler was the dictator of the <u>Soviet</u> <u>Union</u>.

3.018 _____ Douglas <u>MacArthur</u> was in command of the U.S. army in the Philippines at the beginning of the war and military governor of Japan after it.

3.019 _____ The <u>Holocaust</u> was the murder of millions of ordinary people, especially Jews, in Nazi Germany.

3.020 _____ Franklin <u>Roosevelt</u> was the president blamed for the Great Depression.

3.021 _____ World War II began when Germany attacked <u>France</u>.

3.022 _____ <u>El</u> <u>Alamein</u> was the turning point for the war in Europe.

3.023 _____ <u>The</u> <u>New</u> <u>Deal</u> ended the Great Depression.

3.024 _____ Germany, Italy, and Japan were called the <u>Central</u> <u>Powers</u>.

3.025 _____ <u>Dwight</u> <u>D.</u> <u>Eisenhower</u> was the supreme commander for the major Allied invasions of Europe.

3.026 _____ The important U.S. ships that survived Pearl Harbor were <u>aircraft carriers</u>.

3.027 _____ George Patton was a famous <u>German</u> general.

3.028 _____ The worst fighting on D-Day occurred at <u>Utah</u> beach.

3.029 _____ Bernard Montgomery was a famous <u>British</u> general.

3.030 _____ The home front helped win the war by <u>quickly</u> <u>producing</u> <u>war</u> <u>goods</u>.

✔	**Teacher check:**	Initials _____	80
	Score _____	Date _____	100

Before you take the LIFEPAC Test, you may want to do one or more of these self checks.

1. _____ Read the objectives. See if you can do them.
2. _____ Restudy the material related to any objectives that you cannot do.
3. _____ Use the **SQ3R** study procedure to review the material.
4. _____ Review activities, Self Tests, and LIFEPAC vocabulary words.
5. _____ Restudy areas of weakness indicated by the last Self Test.

NOTES

NOTES